Lactose Intolerance

A Practical Guide To Living A Healthy Lactose Free-Dairy Free Life

Bowe Packer

TABLE OF CONTENTS

Publishers Notes 4

Dedication 6

How to Use This Book 7

Part I: Introduction To Lactose Free 9

Chapter 1- Diary or Not? 11

Chapter 2- Understanding Lactose Intolerance for Yourself 14

Chapter 3- Are you at Risk? 16

Chapter 4- Learn What You Need to Know About Lactose Intolerance 18

Chapter 5- Are You Suffering? 21

Chapter 6- How to Fix Your Lactose Problem 23

Chapter 7- Living with Lactose Intolerance 26

Chapter 8- How to Eliminate Lactose from Your Diet 30

Chapter 9- Non-Dairy Ingredients in Your Kitchen 32

Chapter 10- The Problems with a Lactose Free Life 34

Part 2: Recipes Without Lactose 47

About The Author

Publishers Notes

Disclaimer

This publication is intended to provide helpful and informative material. It is not intended to diagnose, treat, cure, or prevent any health problem or condition, nor is intended to replace the advice of a physician.

This publication is intended to provide helpful and informative material and help to get you off to a great start of managing and possibly even curing your lactose intolerance.

Please understand, it is not intended to cover every single aspect about lactose intolerance. You will without a doubt run into certain things that I did not. This is the natural process of life.

However, with that said, I did my very best to cover all the aspect of this particular endeavor and I hope you will see that in the chapters of this book.

Kindle Edition 2013

Manufactured in the United States of America

DEDICATION

I dedicate this book to all those people out there who remind us of the things we have forgotten about ourselves.

And this holds especially true of my beautiful and amazing wife, Alma. She is the one woman who has the most amazing talent to let me grow and love the things about myself that I have not fully accepted.

I cherish the love she has for me when I may not know how to love myself.

May we all have this kind of beautiful soul in our life.

Sent from LOVE,

Sunshine In My Soul

HOW TO USE THIS BOOK

If you are lactose intolerant of if you think that getting rid of dairy out of your life will make you a healthier person (which a lot of people do) then this is the book for you. You may not realize that dairy is causing problems in your diet but chances are that it most definitely is. Even if you aren't allergic to dairy or experiencing problems (that you know of) your body may actually be better off when you cut out dairy products.

Throughout part one of this books we'll talk about ways that you can change your life by getting rid of the dairy products that you eat. That means getting rid of milk, cheese, yogurt and many other products you may eat on a regular basis. But that doesn't mean you have to give up the foods you love because we'll help you find some alternatives to those dairy products so you can still cook, bake and snack without having to worry.

I've only recently switched to a lactose-free diet myself but I have a lot of great things to say about it and a lot of great benefits that I've experienced. If you're interested in learning more about those benefits and how you can experience them too then I definitely suggest reading this book. You'll learn how your body reacts to lactose and how it will react when that lactose is gone as well.

Learn whether or not you have a lactose intolerance and then find out how to combat it. Getting rid of dairy isn't as hard as you may think. We'll show you all about the excellent recipes you can still enjoy in part two of this book. That's where we've included some of my personal favourite recipes that use absolutely no lactose and still taste great.

PART I: INTRODUCTION TO LACTOSE FREE

Personally I love dairy products. I always did. My parents and my siblings love them too. That means that no, I was not born lactose intolerant and I did not have any problems with dairy until I was almost thirty. At that point I started experiencing cramps and pain after meals. For a short time I ignored the problem (not really a good thing to do) but after a while I went to see my doctor and found out that I had a lactose intolerance.

My doctor informed me that eating anything with lactose would trigger some gastric problems such as the cramps and pain I had been experiencing. He said that it was okay to take in just a little dairy (but not very much) though I should be prepared for the outcome after I did. The best option was simply to get rid of dairy from my diet altogether but that was going to be easier said than done since I loved warm milk and oatmeal with milk as well.

My first thought was that I was going to absolutely hate living without dairy products because, after all, what was I going to eat? Nearly everything had some form of dairy or lactose in it. Not only that but the few foods that didn't were all weird right? At least that's what I thought when I first left my doctor's office with the news. I was devastated. This was going to be a huge (and awful) change.

My second thought was that I wasn't going to let this problem get me down. I was going to do some research and find out what I could and couldn't eat. Then I was going to start changing my diet. It didn't take long to decide that cutting out all lactose was the best way to go. I didn't want to deal with the health problems I'd had before going to the doctor so I braced myself for some big changes.

CHAPTER 1- DIARY OR NOT?

How many people do you know that don't drink any milk at all - ever? Chances are that there aren't very many. That's because people drink milk with their meals all the time, they use it in coffee, cereal and oatmeal, they use it to bake cakes and cookies. It's almost impossible to imagine your life without milk but for those with lactose intolerance it's something that you absolutely need to do.

Now if you're one of those people who hasn't been diagnosed with lactose intolerance but you think that getting rid of milk and other dairy products would help change your life for the better then you should definitely talk with your doctor about it. Changing your diet so drastically could actually cause you problems initially and that's why you should always inform your doctor before making changes to your eating habits.

Once you've talked to your doctor about your experiences and problems and the both of you have decided that trying a lactose-free diet might just be the trick it's time to start working on changing your diet.

The first thing to understand is that I have been where you are now. I used to love dairy products and couldn't imagine giving them up but I was able to do it and not only that but I was able to find some excellent tasting foods without lactose in them. Better still, I was able to get rid of my stomach problems completely because I eliminated lactose from my diet.

For some people lactose intolerance is simply part of growing up. It may seem strange but your body could simply decide to stop producing the proper enzyme that allows it to break down milk and give you the benefits you need. Instead, that milk just sits in your stomach and starts irritating the inside of your body which starts the pain and indigestion.

You may be wondering just how you're going to get all the vitamins and minerals that you need in your diet without drinking milk. After all you've probably been told since you were young that Vitamin D comes from milk and it's the only way to help your bones and teeth grow strong. Of course it's true that there is Vitamin D in milk and it's also true that Vitamin D helps make your bones and teeth strong. What's not true is that milk is the only place to get that Vitamin D.

The absolute best way to get Vitamin D however is actually from the sun. Yep that's right being outside actually provides you with 100% natural Vitamin D. All you need to do is spend some time outside though it's important to use proper sunscreen so you don't get too much of the harmful rays.

So what about the rest of the vitamins and minerals found in milk? Well Vitamin C and also many other vitamins are found in fortified orange juices. That means all you need to do is drink one glass of orange juice each day and you're on your way to getting all the vitamins and minerals that you need just like you would get in milk.

Vitamin B is essential for protecting the body against many diseases including Alzheimer's. The great thing is that there are plenty of places you can get Vitamin B that aren't dairy related. These are not only a variety of different vegetables (especially green, leafy ones) but also in nuts and dietary supplements.

CHAPTER 2- UNDERSTANDING LACTOSE INTOLERANCE FOR YOURSELF

So let's start out by explaining what lactose is and what lactose intolerance really is so you can figure out for sure if you have it (though honestly only your doctor can diagnose you). Still this will help you to better understand the reasons for avoiding lactose in your diet whether you have the intolerance or not.

Lactose is a sugar found in milk produced by mammals. That means goat milk, cow's milk, etc. all have lactose in them. This sugar is not able to be digested in its natural form by the human body. In order to be digested it has to be split into different components (glucose and galactose). If it isn't split then the lactose is not digested and the body tends to rebel. That's when you experience the health problems such as pain.

In your body is an enzyme called lactase that will help to break down the lactose that you ingest into your body. If you don't have enough lactase then the lactose will not be broken down and you develop lactose intolerance. If you keep taking in lactose anyway (like I was doing because I didn't know I was lactose intolerant) your body attempts to pass the lactose (still undigested) through the digestive system.

This lactose, as we said, is actually a type of natural sugar and when it passes through the digestive system it causes diarrhea, bloating, pain and more. That means if you don't have lactase in your body or you don't have enough lactase in your body you need to avoid lactase.

CHAPTER 3- ARE YOU AT RISK?

So who suffers from lactose intolerance? Well the first thing to know is that lactose intolerance comes in a variety of different levels. That means someone may experience problems with lactose or difficult in digesting large amounts of lactose without being completely incapable of diagnosing any lactose. This means you could fit anywhere on that spectrum and it's something to talk with your doctor about before you begin a diet like the one we're going to tell you about.

Something you'll want to know about lactose intolerance is who gets it. Well you may be surprised to learn that European Americans actually have the lowest chance and those of Asian, African, South American or Native American descent will typically have the highest likelihood. Of course that doesn't mean that as a European you won't get it or that as a minority race you will. There are plenty of other factors at play.

Once you know your risk factors it's important to really look at the problems associated with avoiding lactose. There are many of course but the two primary ones will be discussed here:

1. **Consuming enough dairy substitutes to stay healthy**
2. **Avoiding hidden lactose in foods that aren't dairy**

So many foods actually contain lactose that you wouldn't think do. Those are things like white bread and some pasta. You need to make sure that you are then avoiding or severely limiting your intake of these foods as well.

CHAPTER 4- LEARN WHAT YOU NEED TO KNOW ABOUT LACTOSE INTOLERANCE

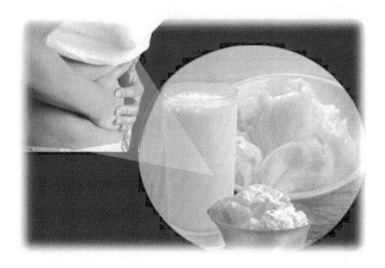

There are many things that you should definitely know about lactose and that's what this section is going to cover. Now some of the points we'll make here are going to be things we've already mentioned but remember that the reason we repeat things is so that you don't fail to remember them. These are all important facts if you are lactose intolerant because they could cause you a lot of harm if you happen to forget them.

1. You must have lactase in order to process lactose.

2. Your body produces the lactase that you need in order to process the lactose that you take into your body.

3. As you get older your body may stop producing as much lactase or it may stop producing it altogether.

4. For most people who develop lactose intolerance it begins quite mild during early adulthood and continues to get worse with age.

5. Symptoms for lactose intolerance range from diarrhea to bloating and also different levels of pain.

6. Some lactose intolerant people can take in small amounts of lactose while others are unable to process any.

7. There may be a genetic link between people that are or become lactose intolerant.

8. Surgery can cause a temporary or permanent level of lactose intolerance depending on the type of surgery that occurs.

9. Temporary lactose intolerance can come about as a result of the flu but disappears when the flu symptoms do.

10. Infants are typically capable of taking in normal amounts of lactose though this is not true of all infants and definitely something to watch out for.

11. Premature children may develop temporary lactose intolerance. This generally goes away as the child starts to get older and their body continues to develop to its normal level.

CHAPTER 5- ARE YOU SUFFERING?

For most people lactose intolerance is not serious or complete. The majority of individuals who suffer from it are only suffering from a form of low lactase production which results in difficulty digesting a lot of lactose. So how does it really work and how can you tell if you are suffering from it?

1. **Symptoms appear approximately ½ hour to 2 hours after consumption of the food containing lactose.**
2. **Acute abdominal pain or cramping**
3. **Gas production and bloating**
4. **Gurgling in the stomach**
5. **Flatulence**
6. **Diarrhea**
7. **Vomiting**

To test if you are actually experiencing lactose intolerance you could go to your doctor or you could attempt a removal of lactose containing ingredients from your diet for a period of one day. If you don't notice any change then chances are you are not actually experiencing lactose intolerance but something different. If this does cause a change then you likely do have some type of intolerance.

No matter what the results of your little test you will want to talk with your doctor. If you realize the symptoms improve without lactose then you want your doctor's approval to go on a lactose free diet and also to get advice on what you should supplement your diet with when removing dairy.

If the symptoms persist without dairy products then you want to make sure that you are talking with your doctor to find out what the problem could be and to reach an accurate conclusion, diagnosis and treatment plan as quickly as possible.

CHAPTER 6- HOW TO FIX YOUR LACTOSE PROBLEM

So how are you going to cure your problem? Well unfortunately for the many who suffer from some level of lactose intolerance there actually is no way to completely cure the problem. All you can do is treat the symptoms and attempt to avoid lactose as much as possible in your diet. So how are you going to do that?

Let's start with the good part of this diagnosis; it's not going to kill you. That may sound a little overdramatic but it is true. You will not die because you are not taking in dairy products (though you could experience problems if you do not supplement your diet in some way to get the vitamins and minerals you need).

Now you'll want to talk with your doctor about the many things you need to do and start thinking about in order to get the changes that you want in your diet and avoid the negative symptoms that you have likely been experiencing. What your doctor will tell you is actually quite simple to follow. Stop eating products that contain lactose in any amount and start taking supplements that will provide you with the things you need.

If you go to your doctor right away with your symptoms then checking for lactose intolerance is likely one of the first things that your doctor will do. They will ask you to avoid high dairy content foods like butter or milk for a period of a couple of days. They will then monitor the results that you experience so that they can determine whether you have lactose intolerance of some type or some level.

There are several different ways that your doctor can help you to determine if you are lactose intolerant that actually don't have to do with checking your symptoms. These are each described below:

1. Blood Sugar Test-This test enables the doctor to measure the level of sugars in your blood stream. What you do is fast for a period of several hours and then drink a high lactose fluid. Your doctor will then perform blood tests over a period of hours to determine how well your body processes the lactose (or neglects to process it) to determine whether you have lactose intolerance. If your body processes the

lactose your blood sugar will increase, if not, your blood sugar will remain the same.

2. Breathe Test-By checking the level of hydrogen in your breath your doctor will be able to tell you whether you are suffering from lactose intolerance. This occurs after a period of selective fasting and the doctor gives you a high lactose liquid that you are to take into your body. Over time the level of hydrogen present in your breath will allow the doctor to determine if you are experiencing the symptoms of lactose intolerance. Though not capable of being performed on infants this type of testing is actually very effective on young adults and older adults.

CHAPTER 7- LIVING WITH LACTOSE INTOLERANCE

So what do you do when you find out you need to switch to a lactose free diet? Well the important thing is to make sure that you follow a slow change. You will likely experience some negative side effects from changing your diet if you do so all at once. You will likely also experience some side effects if you choose not to immediately stop taking in lactose however these side effects are mild in comparison. So what do you do?

1. Lactose intolerance still typically allows you to take in some lactose (10,000 milligrams in 24 hours) though not very much. The limit is generally about one full glass of milk or a similar amount of most lactose containing foods. Just for your information there are many foods with lactose that you can eat in small quantities as long as you keep in mind how much lactose is in each of them.

   - 8 fluid ounces of yogurt-up to 15 grams of lactose
   - 8 fluid ounces of ice cream-up to 10 grams of lactose
   - 30 grams of hard cheese-1 gram of lactose
   - 8 fluid ounces of cottage cheese-3 grams of lactose
   - 1 ounce of cream cheese-0.8 grams of lactose

2. Eating dairy products without other, non-dairy foods will likely cause your symptoms to be worsened. It's important to make sure that you are only adding the dairy product into your meal as a small snack instead of as a snack by itself.

3. Make sure that you look at nutrition labels before you eat anything. Some foods will have a lot of lactose in a small amount. You want to make sure you know if lactose is present in the foods you eat (even if you don't believe there is always check) and how much is in each serving of the food that you eat. Make sure you only eat the correct serving size or number of servings for the amount of lactose you can process.

4. Reduce products that contain lactose within your diet. Use lactose free replacements instead of the more common dairy products.

5. Eliminate the one source of lactose that you consume in any day. This may be milk so get rid of the regular milk and replace it with soy instead. You probably won't notice a whole big difference in taste and you can use the soy milk anywhere you would use regular milk including in your cereal.

6. There are lactase supplements available on the market which can assist lactose intolerant individuals in consuming some amounts of lactose. These supplements may need to be consumed before eating

the lactose or may be added into the lactose containing product before you consume it.

7. Yogurt and milk that is probiotic or has live probiotic bacteria may actually be possible for you to consume without all the negative side effects. Yogurt is very good for you and primarily only the pasteurized yogurt will give the most problems to those with lactose intolerance.

Chapter 8- How to Eliminate Lactose from Your Diet

All right so now you need to start thinking about going lactose free. You need to understand that this means looking at the ingredients list of every food product you buy no matter how likely you think it is that the food contains lactose. You will probably be surprised at the many things that do.

So how do you start the switch? Go home and open up your cupboards and your fridge. You need to make sure that you're getting rid of as much of the dairy filled products that you possibly can. Of course if your family is not going to join you on this dairy free diet you may want to leave some things but try to encourage them to at least try it with you for a little while before returning to their normal diet.

So what should you be looking for in your kitchen that needs to be thrown out?

- ➤ Milk
- ➤ Cheese

- Yogurt
- Ice Cream
- Butter/Margarine
- Cream

All of these ingredients can cause negative symptoms in your body if you consume them and it won't hurt your family to try new alternatives to these things either. So give away or throw away all of your primary dairy ingredients and get ready to start a completely new diet.

CHAPTER 9- NON-DAIRY INGREDIENTS IN YOUR KITCHEN

So here's where it all really begins. How do you cook without using dairy products? Well there's no worries at all actually because everything you need for lactose free living is a lot easier to get then you probably ever thought it would be. What you really need to do is start looking at all the alternatives to dairy that are actually available.

Around the world there are several countries that don't use a lot of dairy products in theirs foods at all. In fact, many countries may not use any dairy in their cooking. That means there are plenty of types of food that you won't have to change at all. And the foods that do use dairy you won't have to change too drastically.

There are several different alternatives to milk that you can choose that can still be used in the same ways that you would use milk. In fact you might be surprised if you walked over to the milk alternatives aisle and really checked out all your options. There are soy versions as well as nut based versions of milk that only taste slightly different and will still be great in your cereal or by the glass.

CHAPTER 10- THE PROBLEMS WITH A LACTOSE FREE LIFE

Now when you think about switching to a lactose free diet it's hard enough but what about when your family *isn't* lactose intolerant? Well if you are switching to a new diet but your family isn't then you could experience even more problems and even more difficulty. Important to know however is that this is still not impossible. It just means you need to be more careful.

In the next couple sections we'll talk about ways that you can go about avoiding lactose foods and dairy products without hindering your family's diet or without getting sucked into a lactose inclusive diet. You don't want to suffer the side effects of ingesting lactose so let's make it a little easier to avoid in your own home.

Everyday Problems

1. Use dairy substitutes wherever possible when you are cooking. These could be in appetizers, salads or even in entrees that you cook for you or your entire family. It won't hurt anyone to try out some lactose free foods every once in a while and they may even find they enjoy it.

2. Change your cooking style to fit your new lifestyle. You may be used to adding milk or cheese to everything that you cook or your spouse may be. Well if that's the case then you're going to need to start rethinking the way that you cook foods and the way you add in special ingredients. You may choose to add in a milk substitute such as soy milk or you may get rid of the extra cheese altogether.

You don't want to use a lot of dairy and lactose products in your cooking simply because it's what you're used to. Don't sacrifice your health for that old flavour you used to like. You'll find something new that makes your food taste just as good or even better than the old one.

So how are you going to make your old favorite foods friendly to your new lifestyle? The first thing you need to do is start researching. Look up alternatives to normal dairy products. You'd be surprised how many books and websites are devoted to exactly that and you'd probably be surprised exactly how many alternatives you really have to choose from.

3. How do you get away from cheese? It's everywhere right? You eat it on sandwiches and in pasta. It's on salads and even some soups. Cheese is literally everywhere you look. So how do you avoid it? Well the best thing for you in this case is to switch to vegan cheese.

Vegans are individuals who not only don't eat meat (vegetarians) but also don't eat any product that comes from an animal. So these are people who do not eat eggs, milk or even cheese. Vegan cheese therefore, comes from oils rather than from an animal. For you that means it doesn't contain dairy and it's safe for you to eat even if you're lactose intolerant.

4. You don't need to get rid of everything you like because you're lactose intolerant. Instead, what you

really need to do is start looking for substitutions that you can make. Trade out the high lactose foods and ingredients for those that don't contain lactose and you'd be surprised how great your food still tastes.

5. Are you still having trouble when you think about all the foods that you have to give up? Well if you are then there's something else you should think about and that's your health. Dairy products are good providers of calcium which is definitely very healthy for you however they are typically good providers of salt, fat and cholesterol also which are definitely too much in abundance in your life.

When you stop eating so much diary you get rid of a lot of the unhealthy additives that you definitely don't need. What you do need are lean meats, veggies, and fish. Those things are still allowed on your dairy free, lactose free diet so there's no need to worry. You'll be amazed at the great flavors you still achieve without dairy.

6. If you love eating pasta then you want to start looking at the different options you have for toppings or sauce. A lot of the normal ones may be full of cheese and other dairy products so what do you do? Well

there are plenty of alternatives that you may want to try.

A lot of people like using nuts or even oils in their pasta. You can choose any of your favourite nuts and all different types of oil especially olive oil because it adds moisture and it's good for your body in many different ways.

7. Start looking at all of your options and all the different ways that you can substitute other foods and ingredients for those including lactose. You'd be surprised at all the options available if you just start looking.

How Your Family and You Interact

1. Making your family their first lactose free meal may be more difficult than you think. If everyone in your family loves cheese and milk then you're probably going to have a hard time convincing them that they should try something new but it's definitely something to work on. Try to get them to give lactose free foods a try.

Talk with your family about your need for a lactose free diet. Explain to them that you'd really like their support and their help avoiding the symptoms you have when you ingest lactose. Once they understand what you're going through they may be more willing to help. Once they agree to help you can start trying new foods.

Make sure you get everyone's input on new foods. You may really love a dish and find out that your family really doesn't. Try to find lactose free meals that everyone enjoys because there will definitely be plenty of them. It just takes a little bit of experimenting to find the right dishes.

What you really need to do is convince your family that lactose free foods are not a punishment for them. You are not punishing them by taking away cheese and milk from their diet but are actually trying to make yourself healthier. They'll be more likely to give it a try if they know the reason for it.

2. If your family doesn't really seem open to the idea of all those new methods of cooking then try to compromise. Let your family know on what days you're going to prepare meals that are lactose free

and which days they will have foods that contain lactose. On days when the meal of the day contains dairy you'll want to prepare your own food on the side.

The point of preparing dairy meals sometimes is to help your family adjust more easily. After all getting rid of lactose from your diet is difficult enough when you have a reason for it. For your family it's an even more difficult diet to deal with because they have no reason to follow it other than you.

3. What do you do when you eat out? Well there are plenty of cultures (as we mentioned before) that don't use a lot of dairy in their food or even any at all. The best choice would be to try one of these places instead of going to a regular American restaurant so that you can avoid a lot of the dairy products and ingredients in your food.

If you can't choose the restaurants with lactose free cuisine then try to find a lactose free dish at the restaurant your family chooses. You'll be amazed how many options you actually have everywhere you go.

4. What do you do if a friend invites you over? This can be difficult terrain because even if your friend knows of your condition should you expect them to have a lactose free snack available for you? The answer is definitely not. Especially if you're going with a group of friends.

The best option for you in this case is to bring an additional snack for yourself. That doesn't mean that you are the only one that gets to eat that food. You want to make sure you take enough that you are willing to share with your friends. You don't want to be *that person* who takes snacks for themselves but not for anyone else. It's definitely not a good thing to do.

How to Get Calcium without Lactose

So now what do you do about the calcium that your body needs? This is something that you absolutely need to take in at the right levels or you'll start losing strength in your bones and teeth. So what are you going to do about that calcium if you're not taking in dairy products?

There are actually many different ways that you can go about getting the calcium that you need and also getting the strong bones that you need. We have several facts and guidelines that you should definitely know and that you will definitely need to know in order to get the nutrients you need while you are lactose intolerant.

1. Your body does not require calcium as the only way to build up your bones. Of course you will need to get calcium somehow. So how are you going to do that? Well the best way is generally with dairy products but for someone who is lactose intolerant there are several other ways that you can get that calcium such as green leafy veggies or nuts.

2. Eating too much salt is actually a problem for your body. Not only does that salt cause you problems in the way of cholesterol but it also takes away calcium from your body. As you take in calcium and take in salt you actually get rid of the calcium.

What you really want to make sure of is that you're not taking in too much sodium in foods like salsa, cheese, milk, crackers, cookies and more. All of those things you can eat of course but you're going to want to make sure you're not eating too much since the sodium causes a lot of health problems. Make sure you are avoiding phosphorous the same ways as it does many of the same things as sodium.

3. Now when you take in calcium from plants how well does your body take it in? The truth is that your body will not absorb as much through this method simply because it's not able to. Some of the chemicals that are present in the plant as well will keep your body from absorbing the calcium the same way it would get it from other sources. Because of this it's important to ensure that your body is *absorbing* the amount of calcium that you need and not just taking it in.

4. If you really want to keep your bones strong another thing will be quite important as well and that one thing is exercise. You want to make sure you are doing enough weightlifting and resistance training that your bones get a workout. The workout you get should take up at least forty minutes each day for at least four days each week.

If you have trouble with exercising frequently then you want to think about the benefits that you get from exercise. One of those benefits is the calcium in your body. Another benefit is the stronger body. Not only that but you'll also be able to prevent circulation problems and back pain as well.

5. You're also going to need Vitamin D from a source other than milk and other dairy products. So where do you get Vitamin D? You may be surprised to know that you can actually get this great vitamin simply by going outside and going into the sun. All it takes is just sitting outside for a few hours a day to absorb Vitamin D to help your bones get stronger than ever.

Where to Find Calcium Without Dairy

If you're lactose intolerant the biggest problem is actually going to be getting calcium. That's because a lot of calcium is obtained through dairy products in a normal diet. Luckily for you however that's not the only place that you can get calcium. It's also in these great (non-dairy) products as well.

Source	Amount of Calcium
Artichoke (medium-sized)	25 milligrams
8 ounces lentils	38 milligrams
Almond butter (1 tbsp.)	43 milligrams
Tortilla (6-inch)	45 milligrams
Wheat bread (2 slices)	60 milligrams
Orange (medium-sized)	61 milligrams
8 ounces broccoli	62 milligrams
8 ounces garbanzos	77 milligrams
Blackstrap molasses (1 tbsp.)	82 milligrams
8 ounces kidney beans	87 milligrams
8 ounces kale	94 milligrams
1 ounce sour cream (vegan/non-dairy variety)	100 milligrams
8 ounces pinto beans	103 milligrams
8 ounces mustard greens	104 milligrams
4 ounces dried figs	121 milligrams
8 ounces navy beans	123 milligrams
8 ounces baked beans	126 milligrams
Tahini (2 tbsp.)	128 milligrams
8 ounces bok choy	158 milligrams
8 ounces soy cheese	183 milligrams
84 grams salmon	188 milligrams

8 ounces almond milk (fortified variety)	*200 milligrams*
28 grams soy cheese (fortified variety)	*200 milligrams*
8 ounces turnip greens	*209 milligrams*
8 ounces collard greens	*266 milligrams*
16 ounces yogurt (soy-based)	*299 milligrams*
8 ounces orange juice (fortified variety)	*300 milligrams*
8 ounces rice milk (fortified variety)	*300 milligrams*
8 ounces soy milk (fortified variety)	*300 milligrams*
4 ounces tofu	*434 milligrams*

PART 2: RECIPES WITHOUT LACTOSE

If you're just getting started with lactose free living then chances are you don't have a lot of recipes to start out with. If you're like most people then you're probably also thinking that you can't possibly have any good food ever again now that you're eliminating lactose from your diet. Well that's absolutely not true at all and that's why we've created this section of our guide. In this chapter you'll learn a lot of new recipes (that taste great). So you'll be able to try something new, start experimenting and enjoy your food without suffering from the side effects of lactose.

Baked Chicken with Thyme

Ingredients:

- 8 ounces soy milk (plain variety)
- Apple cider vinegar (1 tbsp.)
- 16 ounces bread crumbs (check the ingredients for lactose content)
- Fresh/dried thyme (1 tbsp.)
- Salt (1 tsp.)
- Pepper (1/4 tsp.)
- 2 ounces parsley
- Nutritional yeast (2 tbsp.)
- Filleted chicken breasts (4 medium-sized pieces)
- Egg whites from two fresh eggs

Steps:

1. You will need a medium-sized baking pan for this recipe. Apply some non-stick spray on the baking pan and preheat your oven to 400 degrees Fahrenheit.

2. In a non-reactive bowl, mix together the apple cider vinegar and the plain soy-based milk. Let this mixture stand for at least five minutes. You will know when the mixture is ready when the consistency changes. It will thicken -- don't worry!

3. Combine the rest of the ingredients in another non-reactive bowl. Mix well.

4. When the first mixture has thickened, add the egg whites. Make sure you've already beaten the fresh egg whites *before* adding to the thickened vinegar-soy milk mixture.

5. Coat the chicken breasts in the resulting mixture. After coating the chicken breasts in the liquid mixture, coat the fillets in the second mixture (dry mix). Lightly shake the chicken breasts to remove any excess bread crumbs. Light coat the breast fillets with olive oil or any vegetable oil.

6. Place the coated fillets in the prepared baking pan and bake the chicken for at least thirty minutes. If you want the fillets to be extra brown and crispy, you can

bake the entire batch for forty minutes at a consistent 400 degrees Fahrenheit.

Beef Strips with Soy Yogurt

*This recipe is an adaptation of the more common stroganoff recipe cooked around the country (and around the world).

Ingredients:

- *24 ounces of beef strips (any cut will do)*
- *Pepper, ground (1 tbsp.)*
- *Salt (1 tsp.)*
- *4 ounces of olive oil*
- *16 ounces of button mushrooms*
- *Flour (2 tbsp.)*
- *4 ounces of beef broth*
- *5 ounces of yogurt (soy-based)*
- *5 ounces of milk (soy-based)*
- *Dijon mustard (1 tbsp.)*
- *Egg noodles (9 ounces)*
- *Parsley*
- *1 cup of egg noodles (wide variant)*

Steps:

1. Coat the strips of beef with the ground pepper and salt. Pour the olive oil (extra virgin, if available) on a pan or skillet and turn up the heat to medium-high.

2. Cook the strips of beef until desired doneness. The minimum cooking time for thawed beef is seven minutes. Flip the beef strips once or twice to preserve the juices.

3. After cooking the beef strips remove the strips and transfer the meat to a plate. Add some extra virgin olive oil once again to the pan and cook the sliced mushrooms for a few minutes. When the mushrooms have been sautéed to your satisfaction, remove the pan from the fire and let the mushrooms cool a bit.

4. Pour the remaining olive oil in a pan. Add some flour to the olive oil and combine the two with a whisk. When the flour and oil have combined satisfactorily, pour in the beef broth.

5. Add the soy-based yogurt, soy-based milk, and the mustard. Continue mixing until a thick consistency is achieved. Flavor the resulting mix with some salt and ground pepper.

6. The beef stroganoff is now ready. To serve this delectable dish, simply place some noodles on a plate and toss the noodles with some EV olive oil and some chopped parsley. Place a few strips of beef on top of the tossed wide egg noodles. Pour the thick, creamy sauce on top of the beef strips afterward. Serve warm.

Tasty Dumplings

Ingredients:

- *Extra virgin olive oil (2 tbsp.)*
- *Onion (medium-sized, chopped)*
- *Celery stalks (chopped, medium-sized stalks)*
- *Garlic clove (crushed & chopped)*
- *Carrots (4 medium-sized pieces, sliced into strips)*
- *Thyme (1 tsp.)*
- *13 ounces flour*
- *15 ounces chicken stock*
- *2 pounds chicken thigh (deboned and filleted)*
- *Baking powder (1 tbsp.)*
- *Milk powder (soy-based; 1 tbsp.)*
- *Baking powder (1 tbsp.)*
- *Salt (3/4 tsp.)*
- *Margarine (soy-based; vegetarian shortening can also be used; 2 tbsp.)*
- *Egg white (beat the egg white with a whisk)*
- *Salt*
- *Ground pepper*
- *8 ounces milk (soy-based)*

Steps:

1. Sauté 2 tablespoons of extra virgin olive oil, chopped onions, chopped celery stalks, sliced carrots, and dried thyme in a stockpot. Sauté the mixture for at least four minutes. When the initial mix has been sautéed satisfactorily, add 2 tablespoons of flour.

You will know when the new mix is ready when the flour begins to smell slightly nutty from the heat. This should take no more than 45 seconds.

When the flour smells slightly nutty from being cooked, it is now time to add the chicken broth. Alternatively, you can add some tasty vegetable broth. Always use the whisk when mixing the ingredients.

2. To make the batter for this recipe: In a non-reactive mixing bowl, combine 2 tablespoons of baking powder, the rest of the flour, the milk powder (soy-based), and salt. Add the margarine (soy-based, too!) and use a hand-held mixer until the consistency changes from loose to slightly chunky.

In another bowl, combine the beaten egg white and the milk (soy-based). Add the third mixture to the second mixture and slowly combine using a whisk. Dip the chicken pieces into the batter and coat with the second mixture. Fry until desired doneness is achieved.

Amazing Enchilada

Ingredients:

- Enchilada sauce (check for lactose content before using)
- Tortillas (8 pcs., corn-based)
- Cilantro (2 ounces, chopped)
- Cashew nuts (4 ounces, chopped/ground)
- Green bell pepper (chopped)
- Onion (medium-sized, chopped)
- Chicken breasts (deboned and filleted)
- E.V. olive oil (2 tbsp.)
- Salt (1/2 tsp.)
- Garlic powder (1/2 tsp.)
- Tahini (1 tbsp.)
- Salsa (4 ounces)
- Nutritional yeast (4 ounces)
- Almond milk (16 ounces)
- Corn starch (1 tbsp.)

Steps:

1. Preheat your oven to 350 degrees Fahrenheit.

2. In a non-reactive mixing bowl, dissolve 1 tablespoon of corn starch with two tablespoons of almond-based milk. When the cornstarch has been dissolved, proceed to add the rest of the almond-based milk, chopped/ground cashew nuts, 4 ounces of nutritional yeast, salsa, and the rest of the spices and ingredients.

Cook this large mixture for a few minutes until a thick consistency is achieved. This should take no more than 3 minutes. Turn off the heat and let the mixture rest for a few minutes.

3. Pre-heat another pan and cook the chicken. Use E.V. olive oil for frying (or if this isn't available, canola oil will do). Add some chopped onions and chopped bell peppers to the mix.

Fry the chicken for 7 minutes (the minimum cooking time for chicken that has already been thawed out). Remove the chicken from the pan and pat away extra oil from the surface of the chicken. Slice the chicken into 1-inch pieces. Add the chicken to the first mixture, stirring slowly.

Place the chicken mix on the tortillas and proceed to roll the tortillas. Be sure to 'lock' the ends of the tortillas. Place the rolled tortillas in a baking dish and cook for twenty minutes uncovered. Pour on the prepared enchilada sauce. Serve warm.

Vegan Curry Tofu

Ingredients:

- *15 ounces of commercial tofu (sliced into 2-inch pieces)*
- *4 ounces of coconut (shredded)*
- *Cayenne pepper (1/2 tsp.)*
- *Sea salt (1/2 tsp.)*
- *Dry mustard (1/8 tsp.)*
- *Turmeric (1/8 tsp., ground)*
- *Coriander (1/2 tsp.)*
- *Cardamom (1/2 tsp.)*
- *Cumin (1/2 tsp.)*
- *Cashews (raw, 2 ounces)*
- *4 ounces milk (either soy-based or almond-based)*
- *8 ounces water*
- *1 large container of coconut milk (about 15 ounces)*
- *12 ounces of rice (brown or white will do)*

Steps:

1. In a deep pan, place 12 ounces of rice, 15 ounces of coconut milk, 8 ounces of water, 4 ounces of milk, salt, and the rest of the spices.

Place the pan on the stove and bring the mixture to a boil. When the mixture begins to boil energetically, lower the temperature so that mixture begins to simmer. Cover the pan and let the rice cook slowly with the spices for at least 30 minutes.

2. When the curry rice has been cooked satisfactorily, loosen the grains of the rice and add the coconut and the tofu. Let everything cook once again for another 20 minutes. Add some cayenne pepper to flavor the dish and serve.

Shrimp & Spinach Risotto

Ingredients:

- *Ground pepper*
- *Lemon zest*
- *Parsley*
- *Margarine (soy-based, 1 tbsp.)*
- *White wine (4 ounces)*
- *8 ounces rice*
- *Onion (medium-sized, chopped)*
- *Half kilogram shrimp (remove the shells and veins)*
- *Extra virgin olive oil (2 tbsp.)*
- *Salt (2½ tbsp.)*
- *8 ounces lemon juice*
- *16 ounces spinach*
- *16 ounces chicken broth*

Steps:

1. Pour the chicken broth in a small pot and let the contents of the pot simmer for a few minutes. In a non-reactive bowl, add the chopped spinach and flavor it with lemon juice. Toss these two ingredients together until all of the spinach has been coated

evenly with the juice. Add one teaspoon of salt to the mix.

2. Cook the shrimp in another pan (use the E.V. olive oil) for about 4 minutes. Don't forget to flip the shrimp so each side is cooked perfectly. When the shrimp is finally cooked, simply transfer them to a clean plate.

3. Sauté the chopped onions in the same pan where the shrimp was cooked. Add some more extra virgin olive oil if needed. When the chopped onions are translucent and are nearly brown, add the rice.

4. Mix the rice in the pan so the oil is evenly distributed throughout. The rice will also become a little crisp. This should take about 4 minutes of constant stirring.

5. Add 4 ounces of wine to the slightly crispy rice mixture. Continue mixing and stirring the rice so the wine will be absorbed more quickly. This phase of the cooking process will be completed once the wine has been absorbed by the rice.

6. Add a 3/4th cup of the chicken broth to the rice. Again, continue mixing the rice until everything has been absorbed. Continue adding the chicken broth until all of the broth has been absorbed. Cook the rice for an additional 20 minutes.

When the rice is finally cooked, it's time to add the cooked shrimp and chopped spinach. Soy margarine can be added as a final flavoring to the dish. Don't forget to grind some pepper on the risotto before serving warm.

Pumpkin & Nutmeg Surprise

Ingredients:

- *Parsley*
- *Cayenne pepper*
- *White pepper*
- *4 ounces of milk (soy-based or almond-based)*
- *4 ounces coconut milk*
- *Sugar (3 tbsp.)*
- *30 ounces of pumpkin puree*
- *16 ounces water*
- *15 ounces vegetable broth*
- *Salt (1-2 tsp.)*
- *Nutmeg (ground, ¼ tsp.)*
- *Ginger (ground, ½ tsp.)*
- *Cinnamon (ground, ¾ tsp.)*
- *Apple (chopped, 8 ounces)*
- *Leeks (chop the white part of the stalks)*
- *Garlic (one clove, chopped)*
- *8 ounces onion (chopped)*
- *Extra virgin olive oil*

Steps:

1. Pour some olive oil in a pot and turn up the heat to medium-high. Sauté the chopped garlic and chopped

onion in the pot. Cook these ingredients for about 4 minutes.

2. Proceed to add the chopped apple, separated leeks, 3 tablespoons of sugar, and the rest of the spices including the salt. Cook for an additional 2 minutes. The leeks should be softened already at this point.

3. When the first mix has been cooked well, proceed to add the tasty broth and the water to the mixture.

4. Cook the dish for a maximum of 20 minutes. Simmer the soup; don't boil it.

5. Pour the mix into the blender in small increments and transform the puree to a smooth, silky paste. Add the almond-based milk or soy-based milk to the puree as you blend everything.

6. Add coconut milk. The idea here is to integrate the milk products as carefully as possible so the final form

of the puree will have a really full flavor that would go well in a soup.

7. Add the blended pumpkin puree to the pot and slowly mix it in. When the desired consistency and appearance has been achieved, turn off the heat and transfer to a bowl. Serve warm.

Tomato with Soy Milk Soup

Ingredients:

- Parsley
- Salt
- Ground pepper
- Sugar (1 tsp.)
- 16 ounces of milk (soy-based)
- 8 ounces vegetable stock
- 56 ounces of peeled tomatoes
- Cayenne pepper (1/4 tsp.)
- Red pepper (ground, ½ tsp.)
- Thyme (1 tsp.)
- Carrot (get a big one for this recipe, chopped)
- Garlic (4 cloves, chopped)
- Onion (medium-sized, chopped)
- Olive oil (1 tbsp.)

Steps:

1. In a medium-sized pan, sauté the chopped onions and chopped garlic. Add the chopped carrots last and let the heat soften the carrot bits for a few minutes.

This should take around 6 minutes. Continue stirring to impart flavor to the base of the dish. You will know when the base of the soup is perfect when everything is sputtering and fragrant.

2. Add all of the canned tomatoes in the pan. Next, pour in the vegetable broth. Simmer the mix for about 20 minutes.

3. Add the spices and the milk to the soup. Pour the cooked soup in a food processor and blend until a smooth consistency is achieved. Add the sugar and cook for an additional 25 minutes.

Garnish with parsley and serve hot when the desired consistency is achieved.

Turkey-Flavored Stuffing

Ingredients:

- *Margarine (soy-based, 2 tbsp.)*
- *Salt*
- *Ground pepper*
- *Thyme (dried, 1 tsp.)*
- *Sage (1½ tsp.)*
- *16 ounces turkey broth*
- *Garlic clove (whole clove, chopped)*
- *2 eggs*
- *Celery stalks (three stalks, chopped)*
- *12 ounces of onion (chopped)*
- *Olive oil (2 tbsp.)*
- *Wheat bread (two loaves, cubed)*

Steps:

1. Preheat your oven to 325 degrees Fahrenheit. Oil a medium-sized baking dish or use non-stick spray.

2. Sauté the chopped garlic and chopped onion in a pan. Use extra virgin olive oil to sauté these ingredients. This should take about 5 minutes.

3. Combine the eggs and the sliced wheat bread cubes. Add the turkey broth to this mixture and sprinkle the spices. If the mixture is too thick or crumbly, add more broth. However, do not add too much broth as this will make the mixture too light and mushy. You wouldn't want the filling to be too mushy as this will affect the flavor.

4. Add the first mixture (the one with onions) and blend the ingredients well.

5. Place the finished mixture into a pre-sprayed baking dish and cover with foil. Add a bit of soy-based margarine on top before baking for 20 minutes (add a parchment cover). After cooking, remove the parchment and cook for another half hour. Serve hot.

Vegan Potato Treat

Ingredients:

- *Salt*
- *Ground pepper*
- *2 ounces broth powder*
- *Tahini (2 tbsp.)*
- *8 ounces milk (soy-based)*
- *Turmeric (1 tsp.)*
- *2 ounces nutritional yeast*
- *Olive oil (2 tbsp.)*
- *Prepared mustard (1 tbsp.)*
- *Gold potatoes (sliced to wedges)*

Steps:

1. Pre-heat your oven to 400 degrees Fahrenheit. Apply some non-stick spray to a large baking dish.

2. Place all of the potato wedges on the pre-sprayed baking tray. Brush the potatoes with some olive oil to

make them extra crisp and tasty. Add some salt and pepper to the potatoes.

3. Bake the salted potato wedges for about 30 to 45 minutes. Turn the wedges once during the entire cooking process so both sides of the wedges are cooked evenly.

4. And now for the sauce. In a small, non-reactive mixing bowl, combine turmeric and the nutritional yeast. Get a small sauce pan and cook the tahini and the soy-based milk.

5. When the second mixture is slowly simmering, add the nutritional yeast and the turmeric. Continue mixing all of the ingredients with a whisk or spoon. Finally, add the broth powder and mustard. Use a whisk for the final mixing.

Continue cooking the sauce until a thick consistency is achieved. Pour over the potato wedges. Serve and enjoy!

ABOUT THE AUTHOR

Hello, my name is Bowe Chaim Packer and I like to see myself as an open, *"**wear my heart out on my sleeve"*** kind of guy.

Some of the most important things to me in my life are:

- Laughing
- Kissing
- Holding hands
- Being playful
- Smiling
- Talking deeply with others
- Being loved
- Loving others
- Changing the world one person at a time (if my presence in your life doesn't make a difference then why am I here?) Hmmmmm, maybe that is a topic for another book. ;-)
- Learning from others (although often times I first resist). However, don't give up on me....
- Sharing ideas (no matter what they might be)
- Learning about others via most forms of contact.
- Traveling — hello, of course — almost forgot one of my favorite pass times.

Remember, LIFE is a journey for each and every one of us. We must never forget the things that are important to us or lose sight of what makes us happy.

19675597R00044

Printed in Great Britain
by Amazon